The Sacred Rose:
A Guide to the Heart's Unfolding

Pocket Sanctuary Series | Volume IV

Blooming • Inner Petals • Feminine Wisdom
The Heart as a Living Sanctuary

The Sacred Rose: A Guide to the Heart's Unfolding
Pocket Sanctuary Series – Volume IV

This Pocket Sanctuary is intended for personal spiritual enrichment and reflection. It is not meant to replace professional, medical, or therapeutic guidance.

Published by Rooted Hound Press
Vienna, New Jersey
rootedhoundpress.com

Cover design by Rooted Hound Press.

Printed in the United States of America.

ISBN #978-1-969687-11-2

First Edition

For the quiet wisdom that unfolds in its own time.

This sanctuary is not meant to be rushed.

You have not come here to learn how to become something new, but to remember what has always lived quietly within you. Like the rose, the heart unfolds in its own time — not by force, not by demand, but through trust in its natural rhythm.

These pages are an invitation to soften without surrendering yourself, to open without abandoning your center, and to rest in the wisdom that comes from lived experience. Nothing here asks you to fix, prove, or explain who you are. You are not broken, late, or behind.

Move through this sanctuary slowly. Return to it when needed. Let what resonates stay, and let the rest pass gently by. The rose opens not because it is told to, but because the moment arrives.

May this be a place where your heart feels safe enough to unfold.

Table of Contents

Section One - The Rose Before It Opens

There is a moment before blooming
when nothing appears to be happening.
The petals are still folded.
The stem holds steady.
The world may think the rose has paused —
but inside, everything is preparing.
May I trust this moment.
May I not rush the opening.
May I honor the quiet intelligence
that knows exactly when to unfold.

Reflection

Before the rose opens, it gathers itself.

This stage is often misunderstood. From the outside, it can look like hesitation, stillness, or delay. But in truth, it is a sacred inward turning — a time when the heart strengthens its center before revealing its softness.

Many women arrive at this stage after years of giving, adapting, enduring, and loving through effort. The heart has learned what it will no longer do, and it has learned what it must protect in order to remain open at all.

The Rose before it opens is not afraid of love. It is discerning. It no longer blooms on command. It no longer opens to be proven worthy. It opens when it is ready — not because it must, but because it can.

1

If you find yourself here, know this: nothing is wrong. You are not behind. You are not withholding. You are listening to a deeper rhythm — one that honors timing over performance and truth over expectation.

This is not retreat. This is preparation.

Affirmation

I honor the wisdom of my heart's timing. I trust the quiet unfolding within me. I am allowed to bloom when I am ready.

Journaling Prompt

Where in my life am I being asked to pause rather than push?

What is quietly forming within me that does not need to be rushed?

Section Two - The Inner Petals

Not every petal opens at once.
Some remain close to the heart,
holding warmth, memory, and truth.
May I honor what opens easily
and protect what opens slowly.
May I remember that tenderness
is not owed to everyone —
and that my heart knows the difference.

Reflection

The inner petals of the rose are not meant for every eye.

They hold the most delicate aspects of the heart — intuition, sensitivity, memory, and truth that has been earned through experience. These petals are not hidden out of fear, but protected through wisdom. They open gradually, revealing themselves only where it is safe to do so.

Many women are taught that openness means accessibility. That love means full exposure. But the rose teaches otherwise. The deepest parts of the heart are revealed through trust, not pressure.

To honor the inner petals is to know when to share and when to remain inward. It is the quiet discernment that recognizes resonance rather than demand. The heart does not close when it chooses care — it refines.

Inner petals are where softness lives without apology. They are where truth rests before it is spoken. They are where love remains whole.

This is not withholding. This is self-respect.

Affirmation

I honor the tenderness within me. I trust my discernment. I allow my heart to open in ways that feel true and safe.

Journaling Prompt

Which parts of my heart feel most tender right now?

Where am I being asked to protect my inner petals with care rather than guilt?

Section Three - Thorns as Sacred Wisdom

The rose does not grow without thorns.
They are not mistakes
or signs of hardness.
They are guardians —
silent, steady, and precise.
May I honor the places
where I learned to protect myself.
May I understand that boundaries
are not the opposite of love,
but one of its deepest expressions.

Reflection

The thorns of the rose are often misunderstood.

They are not symbols of bitterness or defense, but of discernment. They exist not to wound, but to preserve what is tender. Without thorns, the rose would be easily crushed, stripped, or taken before it was ready.

Many women are taught that love requires openness without limits. That boundaries are unkind, unspiritual, or selfish. Yet the rose teaches a different truth: love without protection cannot endure.

Thorns form through experience. They emerge after learning where energy is lost, where tenderness is misused,

5

and where the heart must stand firm in order to remain open at all. They are not erected in anger, but shaped through wisdom.

To honor the thorns is to release guilt around self-protection. It is to recognize that saying no can be an act of love — for oneself and for others. Boundaries clarify where care is possible and where it is not.

Thorns do not close the heart. They allow it to bloom safely.

Affirmation

I honor the wisdom of my boundaries. I release guilt around self-protection. My discernment allows my heart to remain open and whole.

Journaling Prompt

Where in my life have boundaries protected something tender within me?

What might shift if I viewed my limits as wisdom rather than resistance?

Section Four - The Heart as Sanctuary

There is a place within
that does not need to be explained.
A quiet room
where the heart can lay down its weight
and breathe again.
May I return to this place often.
May I treat my heart
as something sacred,
worthy of rest,
worthy of peace.

Reflection

A sanctuary is not a place of escape. It is a place of return.

When the heart becomes a sanctuary, it no longer seeks constant reassurance from the outside world. It learns how to settle within itself, to listen inwardly, and to rest without needing permission. This kind of sanctuary is built slowly, through self-trust and lived wisdom.

For many women, the heart has been treated as a place of service rather than refuge. It has been asked to hold, soothe, adapt, and endure — often without rest. Over time, this can leave the heart feeling depleted rather than sacred.

The rose teaches that the heart must first be a sanctuary for itself.

This does not mean withdrawing from love or life. It means tending to the inner space where truth, intuition, and peace reside. When the heart is honored as sacred ground, relationships shift naturally. Energy is offered more consciously. Love flows from fullness rather than obligation.

A heart that is treated as a sanctuary knows when to open its gates and when to remain still. It welcomes what nourishes and quietly turns away what disrupts its peace.

This is not isolation. This is reverence.

Affirmation

My heart is a sacred sanctuary. I honor its need for rest and truth. I allow peace to live within me.

Journaling Prompt

What helps my heart feel safe, calm, and restored?

How might my life change if I treated my inner world as sacred space?

Section Five — When the Heart Remembers

There is a knowing that does not ask.

A presence that does not need to be summoned.

It waits not beyond the heart, but within it — quiet, whole, and undivided.

May I rest instead of reaching.

May I remember instead of pleading.

May I trust that what I seek has never been separate from me.

Reflection

In many spiritual traditions, prayer has been taught as an act of reaching outward — asking, appealing, or hoping to be heard. While this form of prayer can bring comfort, it often carries an unspoken assumption: that the Divine exists at a distance, and that connection must be earned or requested.

Yet within early Christian mysticism, there exists a quieter understanding.

During my research into the Magdalene tradition and early contemplative Christianity, I encountered the ancient concept of the *Monad* — a word used to describe the indivisible Source, the One from which all things arise. This was not understood as something to call upon or invoke, but as a way of naming unity itself — the underlying oneness that precedes division, hierarchy, or separation.

In this understanding, prayer is not an act of asking God to come closer. It is the act of becoming still enough to remember that God is already present.

Mary Magdalene is often associated with this form of communion — not through doctrine or instruction, but through embodied intimacy. Her closeness to the Divine was not performative or mediated. It arose from presence, devotion, and an unguarded relationship with the sacred that lived within her as much as beyond her.

When prayer becomes remembrance, the heart does not strive. It listens. It rests. It abides.

This does not replace spoken prayer, nor does it diminish faith. It deepens it. Prayer, in this sense, becomes less about words and more about orientation — the gentle turning of the heart toward what it already knows.

The sanctuary of the heart is not empty. It is inhabited.

When the heart remembers this, devotion softens. Trust replaces effort. And communion becomes something lived, not requested.

Affirmation

I rest in the presence that already surrounds and sustains me.
I allow communion to arise through stillness and trust. What
I seek is not distant from me.

Journaling Prompt

When I pray, do I feel myself reaching outward — or settling
inward?

What shifts when I allow prayer to be presence rather than
petition?

Section Six - Love Without Self-Abandonment

Love does not ask
that I disappear.
It does not require
the shrinking of my voice
or the surrender of my truth.
May I love fully
without leaving myself behind.
May devotion arise
from wholeness,
not from sacrifice.

Reflection

Love that requires self-abandonment is not sustainable.

Many women are taught, subtly or directly, that love means giving until there is nothing left. That devotion is proven through endurance, accommodation, or silence. Over time, this creates a quiet fracture within the heart — a split between who one is and who one feels required to be.

The rose offers a different model of love.

It blooms from its center. It does not rearrange its shape to be more pleasing, nor does it diminish itself to remain connected. Its beauty and fragrance arise naturally from wholeness, not from self-erasure.

12

To love without self-abandonment is to remain present with one's own needs, values, and inner knowing while offering care to others. It is the practice of staying rooted in oneself while extending love outward.

This kind of love may feel unfamiliar at first. It can challenge old patterns of over-giving or people-pleasing. Yet it creates relationships grounded in truth rather than obligation.

Love does not ask for disappearance. It asks for presence — whole and intact.

Affirmation

I choose love that honors my wholeness. I remain rooted in myself as I care for others. My love is generous and self-respecting.

Journaling Prompt

Where in my life have I mistaken love for self-sacrifice?

What would it feel like to love while remaining fully present to myself?

Section Seven - The Feminine Art of Letting Go

Letting go does not mean
turning away in anger
or closing the heart in fear.
It is the quiet release
of what no longer belongs.
May I loosen my grip
without hardening my hands.
May I trust that what is meant to remain
will not be lost by gentleness.

Reflection

Letting go is often misunderstood as loss, failure, or withdrawal. Yet the feminine way of release is rarely abrupt or forceful. It is gradual, intuitive, and rooted in discernment rather than reaction.

The rose does not drop its petals all at once. It releases them slowly, when their purpose has been fulfilled. In this way, letting go is not an act of rejection, but of completion.

For many women, holding on has been a form of survival. Roles, relationships, expectations, and responsibilities may have once provided safety or meaning. Over time, however, what was once necessary can become burdensome, asking the heart to carry more than it was meant to hold.

14

The feminine art of letting go is not about pushing away. It is about recognizing when something has finished its season. It is the courage to loosen attachment without needing to justify the release.

Letting go does not erase love. It allows love to change form.

When release is guided by wisdom rather than resentment, it creates space — space for rest, truth, and what wishes to arrive next.

Affirmation

I allow myself to release what has completed its season. I let go with grace and discernment. I trust the space that follows.

Journaling Prompt

What in my life feels ready to be released gently rather than held tightly?

What might become possible if I trusted the wisdom of this letting go?

Section Eight - Blooming Where One Is Planted

I do not need to wait
for perfect conditions
to begin.
The soil beneath me
is enough for this moment.
May I root where I stand.
May I trust that blooming
does not require escape,
only presence.

Reflection

Blooming where one is planted is not about settling. It is about inhabiting the present with honesty and care.

The rose does not choose its location. It grows where it is placed, drawing nourishment from the soil available to it. Even imperfect ground can support growth when tended with attention and patience.

For many women, there is a quiet belief that fulfillment lies somewhere else — another season, another role, another version of life. While change can be necessary, the rose reminds us that meaning is often found not in leaving, but in fully arriving where we are.

To bloom where one is planted is to engage with life as it is, rather than postponing joy or wholeness until conditions improve. It is the practice of offering one's presence, wisdom, and care to the moment at hand.

This does not deny longing or future possibility. It simply honors that growth happens now, in the ordinary rhythms of daily life. When attention is given to what is present, beauty emerges naturally.

· Blooming is not about circumstance. It is about participation.

Affirmation

I choose to be present where I am. I allow growth to unfold in my current season. I trust that blooming begins here.

Journaling Prompt

Where in my life am I being invited to show up more fully right now?

What might change if I stopped waiting for better conditions to begin?

Section Nine - The Rose at Rest

There comes a time
when nothing more is asked.
The petals have opened.
The fragrance has been given.
Now the rose rests
in quiet completion.
May I honor this stillness.
May I trust that becoming
does not require striving.
May I allow myself
to simply be.

Reflection

Every bloom reaches a moment of rest.

After the opening, after the offering, there is a natural settling — a return to simplicity. The rose does not cling to its petals or measure its worth by how long it is admired. It rests, complete in what it has already given.

For many women, rest can feel unfamiliar or undeserved. There is often an urge to keep moving, fixing, or becoming. Yet the wisdom of the rose reminds us that wholeness is not earned through effort alone. It is recognized through presence.

The Rose at Rest is not diminished. It is fulfilled.

This stage invites acceptance — of self, of season, of life as it is. It is the quiet knowing that nothing essential is missing. The heart no longer reaches outward for validation, nor does it retreat inward in fear. It simply resides in itself.

Rest is not the end of growth. It is the integration of all that has been lived.

In this stillness, the rose remains what it has always been — rooted, radiant, and whole.

Affirmation

I allow myself to rest in wholeness. I release the need to strive or prove. I honor the completeness of this moment.

Journaling Prompt

Where in my life am I being invited to rest rather than reach?

What would it feel like to trust that I am already enough?

Section Ten - Tending the Rose Daily

I do not need
grand rituals
or perfect devotion.
A moment is enough.
A breath.
A hand to the heart.
May I tend what is living
within me
with simplicity
and care.

Reflection

The rose does not require constant attention, but it does require presence.

Tending the rose daily is not about discipline or performance. It is not another task to be added to an already full life. It is a way of moving through the day with awareness — noticing when the heart feels open, when it feels guarded, and when it simply needs rest.

Daily tending can be as simple as pausing before responding, choosing honesty over habit, or allowing softness where hardness once lived. It may look like returning to the breath, touching the body gently, or honoring a quiet inner "no."

The feminine way of tending is responsive rather than rigid. It listens first. It adjusts as needed. Some days the rose is vibrant and expressive. Other days it is quiet, folded inward, conserving energy. Both are expressions of life.

To tend the rose is to stay in relationship with oneself. It is the ongoing practice of remembering that the heart is alive, changing, and worthy of care — even on ordinary days.

Devotion does not need to be dramatic. It only needs to be sincere.

Affirmation

I tend my inner life with gentleness and respect. I listen to what my heart needs each day. My presence is enough.

Journaling Prompt

What simple practices help me stay connected to my heart?

How can I offer myself care without turning it into obligation?

Section Eleven - Carrying the Rose Forward

I do not place the rose down
when the pages end.
I carry it quietly
into my days,
my choices,
my becoming.
May what has opened
continue to unfold.
May what has softened
remain strong.
May I walk forward
with the wisdom
I now hold.

Reflection

The rose does not end when the book closes.

What has been opened here is not meant to stay contained within these pages. It is meant to move with you — into conversations, decisions, pauses, and moments of return. Carrying the rose forward is not about remembering every word, but about living the essence of what has been felt.

This sanctuary has offered a way of relating to the heart — with discernment, reverence, and trust. As you move forward, the rose may appear in subtle ways: a boundary held with kindness, a release made without regret, a moment of rest chosen over striving.

There is no finish line to this path. The rose continues to bloom, rest, and renew itself through seasons. Carrying it forward simply means honoring the wisdom you now recognize as your own.

You do not need to seek the rose again. It already lives within you.

Let this knowing accompany you gently, without pressure or expectation. The unfolding will continue, just as it always has — in its own time, in its own way.

Affirmation

I carry this wisdom with me into my life. I trust the unfolding that continues beyond these pages. What I have received is already part of me.

Journaling Prompt

What insights from this sanctuary feel most alive for me right now?

How might I carry this wisdom forward in small, meaningful ways?

*9 7 8 1 9 6 9 6 8 7 1 1 2 *